Kelbourne Woolens

BABY COLLECTION

Kate Gagnon Osborn + Courtney Kelley

First edition.

ISBN 978-0-9895488-0-9

Printed in the United States by Puritan Press on FSC-certified papers using vegetable-based inks.

Knitting: Grace Anna Farrow, Courtney Kelley, Deidre Kennedy, Kate Gagnon Osborn

Writing: Courtney Kelley, Kate Gagnon Osborn

Technical Editing: Kate Gagnon Osborn, Laura Grutzeck

Photography: Amanda Stevenson + Jen Bragan

Graphic Design: Kate Gagnon Osborn

Yarn and Pattern Support: Contact info@kelbournewoolens.com for inquiries on patterns or The Fibre Company yarns. Online, keep up-to-date with Kelbourne Woolens on Facebook or through kelbournewoolens.com/blog. Additionally, please join the Kelbourne Woolens and I Heart The Fibre Company groups on Ravelry.com to share your projects, comments, and pattern questions with knitters worldwide.

Table of Contents

Introduction:

In the beginning...there was a swatch.

Or, more accurately, there ought to be a swatch. We are ardent swatch knitters and swatch washers. We not only knit swatches, we encourage you to treat the swatch the way you will be treating your garment in real life. Knit your swatch in the stitch pattern called for in the design, either flat or in the round as called for in the pattern. Wash your swatch, give it a little tug, let it dry, and steam it. This will not only give you a more accurate finished gauge, but it will give you a glimpse of the future of your garment. Measure your swatch over at least four inches. Many of our swatches are as large as 6–10" squares. It can be frustrating to take what is seemingly wasted time to do so, especially when you are eager to cast on a new project, but why bother to cast on 145 stitches only to realize that you hate the way the yarn knits up or that your adorable sweater for a newborn baby won't fit until the little tyke is 4 years old?

Choosing Yarns: We consider ourselves incredibly lucky to have so much fantastic yarn at our fingertips. While swatching can tell you a lot about how your project will turn out, choosing a good yarn at the start is half the battle. Whenever possible, we encourage you to work with the recommended yarn in the pattern to get the same look, drape, and feel as the original. If this is not possible, choosing a yarn that contains a similar fiber blend is best. Choose yarns with care, and choose yarns you love - your time and effort are worth it!

Skill Levels: All the patterns in this collection are designed for an intermediate skill level - not too difficult, not too easy, with enough technique to keep you going, but not too much to make you frustrated.

Reading Charts: When working from a chart, you will work the stitches as they appear, so it's easy to tell if you have gone astray. Not only do charts tell you what to do, they give you a visual representation of what your work should look like. Each square on the chart represents one stitch on your needle, and the symbols tell you what to do with that stitch. Charts are read from the bottom up and from right to left on right-side rows and from left to right on wrong-side rows. In color knitting you'll most likely be working in the round and, in that case, you'll always be reading the chart from right to left. Patterns will have a symbol key if they are utilizing a charted pattern. If you are unsure of what a symbol or abbreviation means, the Internet is a great resource, as is your local library! There are many books with extensive keys, and many of the symbols and abbreviations are fairly standardized. Many people use Post-it notes or removable highlighter tape to help them track which row they're on. There are a lot of nifty gadgets out there, but we like to keep it simple: using a pen to mark our place works perfectly fine!

Finishing and Garment Care: It may seem odd to put this section in the introduction, but it is an important consideration. This is how we wash both our swatches and finished pieces: soak your item in a sinkful of tepid water and a bit of your favorite no-rinse wool wash. Lay the garment flat on a clean, dry towel and roll it up like a jelly roll. Fold the roll once or twice, and kneel on it to squeeze as much water out as possible. If you're working with a finished item, don't tug it too much, but feel free to even out the places that need a little extra care, especially if you have done color work or lace. While the item is still damp, lay it out on a dry towel or blocking board until it is completely dry. Kate pins her items; Courtney does not (unless she absolutely has to.)

We wash our knitted items at least once a year, more often for pieces such as gloves and sweaters that get frequent use. If giving the knitting as a gift, it is always a nice idea to include a care tag with fiber content and washing instructions as well as a few extra yards of yarn and buttons (if applicable) in case the item gets an extensive amount of love and requires darning or button replacement.

Basil

by Courtney Kelley

● ● ○ ○

skill level: intermediate

YARN: The Fibre Company Canopy Fingering (50% baby alpaca, 30% merino, 20% viscose from bamboo; 200 yds/50gm skein): orchid (MC), 3 skeins + aloe (CC): 2 skeins.

GAUGE: 22 sts + 38 rnds = 4" (10 cm) in lace patt on larger ndls, after blocking.

NEEDLES: 1 - 24" or 36" US 3 (3.25 mm) circ + 1 - 24" US 4 (3.5 mm) circ and set dpns, 1 - US 7 (4.5 mm) dpn for bind off.

NOTIONS: 4 stitch markers, tapestry needle.

SIZE: 28.5" square.

SKILLS: Working lace from charts.

Basil

WORTHY OF NOTE: Basil begins from the center out on dpns. You will move to the circular needle when the circumference is too large to fit comfortably on the dpns. Increases are worked every other round. Only ¼ of the blanket is charted. Work charts 4 times across to complete the round. When placing markers, you may find it helpful to use a different (color or type) marker for the beg of the round. When working all lace charts, slip the markers as you come to them.

KEY:

SET-UP CHART:

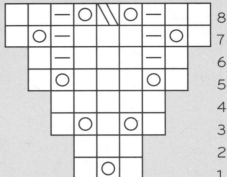

BODY CHART:

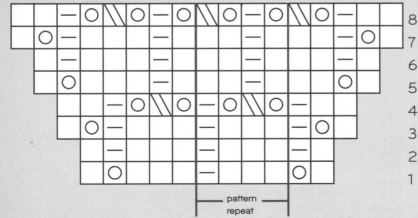

pattern repeat

DIRECTIONS:

BODY: Using MC and size 4 ndls, *CO 2 sts, pm; rep from * 3 times more - 8 sts. Join for working in the rnd, being careful not to twist sts. Work rnds 1-8 of Set-Up Chart - 36 sts. Work rnds 1-8 of Body Chart 15 times - 516 sts.

EDGING: Rnd 1: *K1, m1, p to one st before m, m1, k1; rep from * to end - 8 sts inc'd. Rnd 2: Knit all sts. Repeat rnds 1 + 2 two times more - 540 sts. Change to CC. Rnd 7: *K1, m1, k to one st before m, m1, k1; rep from * to end - 8 sts inc'd. Rnd 8: Knit all sts. Repeat rnds 7 + 8 eleven times more - 636 sts. **Work picot:** Next rnd: K1, *yo, k2tog; rep from * to end. **Work Hem:** Change to smaller ndls. Rnd 1: *K1, k2tog, knit to one st before m, skp, k1; rep from * to end - 8 sts dec'd. Rnd 2: Knit all sts. Repeat rnds 1 + 2 twelve times more - 532 sts.

FINISHING: Bind off all stitches using large dpn, attaching hem to WS of blanket as you go as follows: Insert RH needle into stitch on the LH needle and into the corresponding purl bump on the WS of the blanket, knit together the LH stitch and the purl bump and complete the bind off. Weave in ends. Soak in cool water and wool wash and block to measurements.

Beatrix

by Courtney Kelley

⬤ ⬤ ◯ ◯

skill level: intermediate

YARN: The Fibre Company Acadia (60% merino wool, 20% baby alpaca, 20% silk; 145 yds/50gm skein): sand (MC), 2 (3, 4, 4, 5, 6) skeins + summersweet (CC), 1 skein.

GAUGE: 24 sts + 48 rows = 4" (10 cm) in garter st, after blocking.

NEEDLES: 1 - 24" US 3 (3.25mm) circs and pair straights.

NOTIONS: 1 - 1" button(s), darning needle, 4 stitch markers.

SIZE: NB-6 mos (6-12 mos, 12-18 mos, 2T, 3T, 4T).

SKILLS: Knitting flat, increasing, decreasing, picking up stitches.

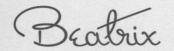

Beatrix

WORTHY OF NOTE: The body of Beatrix is worked flat in one piece beginning at the back hem. Stitches are then held for the neck and the left and right fronts are worked separately. A mitred border + collar is worked on the fronts, sleeves are then worked flat and seamed.

DIRECTIONS:

BACK: Using MC, CO 54 (60, 66, 72, 78, 84) sts. Beginning with a RS row, work in garter st for 16 rows. Change to CC and work in garter st for 14 rows. Change to MC and work in garter st until piece meas 6 (6.5, 7, 7.5, 8.5, 9.5)" from CO edge, ending after working a WS row. **Shape Armholes:** BO 5 (5, 5, 6, 6, 6) sts at beg of next 2 rows - 44 (50, 56, 60, 66, 72) sts. Work in garter st for 2.5 (3, 3.5, 3.75, 4.5, 5.5)" more, ending after working a WS row. **Divide For Neck:** (RS): Knit 12 (15, 16, 18, 20, 21) sts and place on holder, (right shoulder), knit center 20 (20, 24, 24, 26, 30) sts and place on holder, knit remaining 12 (15, 16, 18, 20, 21) sts (left shoulder). Work fronts separately.

LEFT FRONT: Work 10 (10, 12, 14, 14, 16) rows in garter st. **Begin Neck Increases:** Row 1 (WS): K to 1 st rem, m1L, k1 – 1 st inc'd. Row 2: K all sts. Rep rows 1+2 5 (5, 5, 6, 6, 6) times more - 18 (21, 22, 25, 27, 28) sts. Work in garter st to match back to underarm. CO 5 (5, 5, 6, 6, 6) sts at end of next RS row – 23 (26, 27, 31, 33, 34) sts. **Body:** Work in garter st to match back to beg of CC stripe, ending after working a WS row. Place sts on a holder.

RIGHT FRONT: Reattach yarn on WS at neck edge of right shoulder. Work 10 (10, 12, 14, 14, 16) rows in garter st. **Begin Neck Increases:** Row 1 (WS): K1, m1R, knit to end – 1 st inc'd. Row 2: Knit all sts. Rep rows 1+2 5 (5, 5, 6, 6, 6) times more - 18 (21, 22, 25, 27, 28) sts. Work in garter st to match back to underarm. CO 5 (5, 5, 6, 6, 6) sts at beg of next RS row – 23 (26, 27, 31, 33, 34). **Body:** Work in garter st to match back to beg of CC stripe, ending after working a WS row.

BORDER: With RS of Right Front facing and using CC, knit 23 (26, 27, 31, 33, 34) right front sts, pm, pick up and knit 1 st in each garter ridge along right front, pm, pick up and knit 1 st in each garter ridge along neck inc's and shoulder edge, knit 20 (20, 24, 24, 26, 30) sts off holder for back neck, pick up and knit 1 st in each garter ridge along shoulder and neck inc's, pm, pick up and knit 1 st in each garter ridge along left front, pm, knit 23 (26, 27, 31, 33, 34) sts off of Left Front holder. Knit 1 row. **Begin Mitred Corners:** Row 1 (RS): *Knit to 1 st before m, K1f+b, slm, k1f+b; rep from * 3 times more, knit to end – 8 sts inc'd. Row 2 (WS): Knit all sts. Rep rows 1 + 2 five times more. Change to MC. Work Rows 1 + 2 three times, then Row 1 once. **Work Buttonhole:** Next Row (WS): Knit to 3rd m, slm, knit 3.5", BO 4 sts, knit to end. Next Row (RS): Work in patt as set to buttonhole, CO 4 sts over buttonhole, work in patt as set to end – 8 sts inc'd. Work Row 2 once then Rows 1 + 2 twice, then Row 1 once more. Next Row (WS): BO all sts.

SLEEVES: CO 36 (36, 40, 44, 48, 56) sts and work in garter st for 5 (5.5, 6, 6.5, 7.5, 8.5)", ending with a WS row. Dec row: K1, *k2, k2tog; rep from * to 3 sts rem, k3 - 28 (28, 31, 34, 37, 39) sts. Work in garter for .5" more, ending after working a RS row. Change to CC and work in garter for 1". Bind off all sts.

FINISHING: Wet block pieces to measurements. Sew sleeves into armholes. Sew side seams. Sew sleeve seams, leaving 1.5" open at cuff. Turn sweater inside out and sew rem 1.5" of sleeve seam. Turn up cuffs as shown and tack at seam. Sew button to right front.

SCHEMATIC:

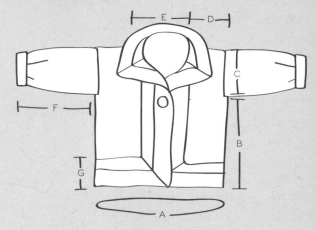

A: 18 (20, 22, 24, 26, 30)"
B: 6 (6.5, 7, 7.5, 8.5, 9.5)"
C: 3 (3, 3.5, 3.75, 4, 4.5)"
D: 2 (2.5, 2.5, 3, 3.5, 3.5)"
E: 3.5 (3.5, 4, 4, 4.5, 5)"
F: 5.5 (6, 6.5, 7, 8, 9)"
G: 2.5"

Cécile

by Kate Gagnon Osborn

skill level: intermediate

YARN: The Fibre Company Terra (60% baby alpaca, 20% alpaca + 20% silk; 98 yds/50gm skein): hollyhock, 3 (4, 4, 5) skeins.

GAUGE: 17 sts + 25 rows = 4" (10 cm) in St st, after blocking.

NEEDLES: 1 - 24" US 7 (4.5 mm) circs or pair straights.

NOTIONS: Tapestry needle, 2 stitch markers, 5 - 3/4" buttons, waste yarn or stitch holder.

SIZE: NB-6 mos (6-12 mos, 12-18 mos, 2T).

SKILLS: Knitting, purling, increasing, decreasing.

Cecile

WORTHY OF NOTE: Cecile is worked in one piece. It begins with a cast-on for back, then knit up to the armholes, cast-on for the sleeves, work 1/2 of the sleeves, then divide and work the remainder of the sleeves and front separately. Stitches are then picked up to work the hood. After seaming, stitches are picked up for the garter buttonband.

DIRECTIONS:

BACK: CO 38 (42, 46, 50) sts. Work in garter stitch for 1.25", ending after working a RS row. Next row (WS): Purl all sts. Next row (RS, inc row): K 8 (9, 9, 10), m1, *k 7 (8, 9, 10), m1; rep from * to 9 (9, 10, 10) sts rem, knit to end - 42 (46, 50, 54) sts. Work in St st until piece meas 6 (6.5, 7.5, 8.75)" from CO edge, ending after working a WS row.

CAST ON FOR SLEEVES: Row 1 (RS): Using backwards loop, CO 6 (6, 7, 8) sts, knit to end. Row 2 (WS): Using backwards loop, CO 6 (6, 7, 8) sts, purl to end. Rep Rows 1 + 2 three times more – 90 (94, 106, 118) sts. Row 9: Sl1, knit to end. Row 10: Sl1, knit 5, purl to 6 sts rem, knit 6. Rep Rows 9 + 10 6 (7, 8, 9) times more. Piece should meas appx. 9.5 (10.5, 11.5, 13.25)" from CO edge.

DIVIDE FOR FRONTS: Row 1 (RS): Sl1, knit 33 (35, 39, 45) sts, place remaining 56 (58, 66, 72) sts on waste yarn, turn. Row 2 (WS): Purl to 6 sts rem, k6.

RIGHT FRONT: Row 1 (RS): Sl1, knit to end. Row 2 (WS): Purl to 6 sts rem, k6. Row 3: Sl1, knit until 2 sts rem, m1R, k2. Row 4: Purl until 6 sts rem, k6. Rep Rows 3 + 4 4 (4, 5, 5) times more - 39 (41, 46, 52) sts. Next row (RS): Sl1, knit to end. Next Row (WS): CO 7 (7, 8, 8) sts using backwards loop, purl until 6 sts rem, k6 - 46 (48, 54, 60) sts. Work straight in patt as set for 0 (0, 2, 4) rows more.

BIND OFF SLEEVES: Row 1 (RS): BO 6 (6, 7, 8), knit to end. Row 2: Purl all sts. Rep Rows 1 + 2 three times more - 22 (24, 26, 28) sts after all BOs have been worked. Work in St st until front meas 4.75 (5.25, 6.25, 7.5)" from final sleeve bind off, ending after working a RS row. Next row (WS, dec row): K6 (7, 7, 8) sts k2tog, k6 (6, 8, 8) sts k2tog, k6 (7, 7, 8) sts - 20 (22, 24, 26) sts. Work in Garter st for 1.25", ending after working a RS row. BO all sts knitwise.

LEFT FRONT: Place 34 (36, 40, 46) left

front + sleeve sts onto ndls, leaving 22 (22, 26, 26) center sts on waste yarn. Join yarn at neck edge. Row 1 (RS): Knit all sts. Row 2 (WS): Sl1, K5, purl to end. Rep Rows 1 + 2 once more. Row 5: K2, m1L, knit to end. Row 6: Sl1, K5, purl to end. Rep Rows 5 + 6 4 (4, 5, 5) times more - 39 (41, 46, 52) sts. Next row (RS): Knit all sts. Next row: Sl1, k5, purl to end, CO 7 (7, 8, 8) sts using backwards loop cast-on - 46 (48, 54, 60) sts. Work straight in patt as set for 1 (1, 3, 5) rows more.

BIND OFF SLEEVES: Row 1 (WS): BO 6 (6, 7, 8) purl to end. Row 2: Knit all sts. Rep Rows 1 + 2 three times more - 22 (24, 26, 28) sts after all BOs have been worked. Work in St st until front meas 4.75 (5.25, 6.25, 7.5)" from final sleeve bind off, ending after working a RS row. Next row (WS, dec row): K6 (7, 7, 8) sts k2tog, k6 (6, 8, 8) sts k2tog, k6 (7, 7, 8) sts - 20 (22, 24, 26) sts. Work in Garter st for 1.25", ending after working a RS row. BO all sts knitwise.

HOOD: Transfer 22 (22, 26, 26) center back sts to spare ndl. Row 1 (RS): Starting at right front, p/u and knit 7 (7, 8, 8) sts across right front, p/u and knit 11 (11, 13, 15) sts along neck edge, knit 22 (22, 26, 26) back sts, p/u and knit 11 (11, 13, 15) sts along

left neck edge and 7 (7, 8, 8) sts across left front cast-on - 58 (58, 68, 72) sts. Row 2 (WS): Purl 19 (19, 22, 24) sts, pm, purl 20 (20, 24, 24) sts, pm, purl to end. **Increase For Neck:** Row 1: Knit to 1 st before m, m1L, k1, slm, k1, m1R, knit to 1 st before m, m1L, k1, slm, k1, m1R, knit to end - 4 sts inc'd. Work straight in St st for 5 rows. Rep prev 6 rows twice more, removing ms as you come to them on last inc row - 70 (70, 80, 84) sts. Work straight until hood meas 4.25 (4.75, 5.25, 6.25)" ending after working a WS row as follows: Purl 35 (35, 40, 42) sts, pm, purl to end. **Decrease For Top:** Row 1: Knit to 2 sts before m, ssk, slm, k2tog, knit to end - 2 sts dec'd. Work 3 rows even. Rep decrease row every 4th row 2 (2, 3, 3) times, then every other row 4 (4, 5, 5) times more - 56 (56, 62, 66) sts. Transfer 28 (28, 31, 33) hood sts to spare circ ndl. Fold top of hood in half and seam using kitchener stitch.

BUTTONBAND: Starting at right front, pick up and knit 30 (36, 36, 42) sts up right front, 60 (64, 76, 84) sts around hood, and 30 (36, 36, 42) sts down left front - 120 (134, 148, 168) sts. Work in garter stitch for 5 rows. **Work Buttonholes:** Next row (RS): Sl-1wyib, k2, yo, k2tog, *k6, yo, k2tog; rep from * 2 (3, 3, 4) times more, knit to end. Work in garter stitch for 4 rows. BO all sts knitwise.

FINISHING: Sew side seam. Sew together arms. Weave in ends. Soak in cool water and wool wash and block to measurements. Sew on 4 (5, 5, 6) buttons opposite button-holes.

SCHEMATIC:

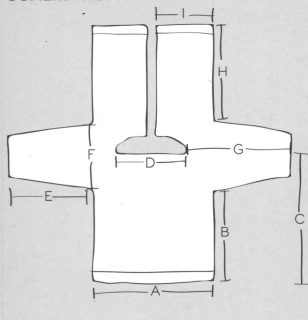 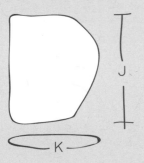

A: 9 (9.75, 10.75, 11.75)"
B: 6 (6.5, 7.5, 8.75)"
C: 9.5 (10.5, 11.5, 13.25)"
D: 5.25 (5.25, 6, 6)"
E: 5.5 (5.5, 6.5, 7.5)"
F: 7 (8, 8, 9)"
G: 8 (8.5, 9.25, 10.75)"
H: 6 (6.5, 7.5, 8.75)"
I: 5 (5.5, 6, 6.5)"
J: 7 (7, 9, 10)"
K: 16 (16, 18, 19.25)"

Clarence

by Courtney Kelley

● ● ○ ○

skill level: intermediate

YARN: The Fibre Company Canopy Worsted (50% baby alpaca, 30% merino, 20% viscose from bamboo; 200 yds/100gm skein): blue quandons, 1 skein.

GAUGE: 22 sts + 32 rows = 4" (10 cm) in St st, after blocking.

NEEDLES: 1 - US 4 (3.5 mm) set dpns.

NOTIONS: stitch marker, waste yarn, tapestry needle.

SIZE: 3.25 (4.5, 5.5, 6.5)" designed to snugly fit 6-12 mos (12-24 mos, 2-4 years, 4-6 years).

SKILLS: Knitting, purling, increasing.

Clarence

WORTHY OF NOTE: Depending on the size you choose to knit, there is enough yarn in one skein of Canopy Worsted to make at least 3 pairs of handwarmers.

RIBBING (IN THE RND): Rnd 1: *K1, p1; rep from * around. Rep rnd 1 for patt.

THUMB INCREASES:
Rnd 1: K1f+b, k1f+b, knit to end - 2 sts inc'd.
Rnd 2 (and all even rnds): Knit all sts.
Rnd 3: K1f+b, k2, k1f+b, knit to end - 2 sts inc'd.
Rnd 5: K1f+b, k4, k1f+b, knit to end - 2 sts inc'd.
Rnd 7: K1f+b, k6, k1f+b, knit to end - 2 sts inc'd.
Rnd 9: K1f+b, k8, k1f+b, knit to end - 2 sts inc'd.
Rnd 11: K1f+b, k10, k1f+b, knit to end - 2 sts inc'd.
Rnd 13: K1f+b, k12, k1f+b, knit to end - 2 sts inc'd.

DIRECTIONS (MAKE 2):
CUFF: Cast on 18 (24, 30, 36) sts.

Divide evenly onto 3 dpns. Join for working in the rnd, being careful not to twist sts. PM indicating beg of rnd. Work in garter st for 3 rnds. Work in Ribbing for 8 (10, 12, 14) rnds. Work in St st for 0 (2, 4, 6) rnds.

BEGIN THUMB INCREASES: Work rnds 1-5 (1-7, 1-9, 1-11) of thumb inc's - 24 (32, 40, 48) sts after all inc's have been worked.

DIVIDE FOR THUMB + HAND: Rnd 1: K1, CO 2 sts using backwards loop method, sl 5 (7, 9, 11) thumb sts onto holder, knit to end - 19 (25, 31, 37) sts. Work in St st on 19 (25, 31, 37) hand sts for 4 (6, 8, 12) rnds. Purl 1 rnd. Knit 1 rnd. Loosely BO all sts purlwise.

THUMB: Transfer 5 (7, 9, 11, 13) thumb stitches onto 2 dpns. Using 3rd dpn, pick up 2 sts in 2 CO sts at base of thumb – 7 (9, 11, 13, 15) sts. Knit 3 (5, 7, 9, 11) rnds. Loosely BO all sts purlwise.

FINISHING: Weave in ends. Soak in cool water and woolwash and block to measurements.

Colette

by Kate Gagnon Osborn

skill level: intermediate

YARN: The Fibre Company Road to China Light (65% baby alpaca, 15% silk, 10% camel, 10% cashmere; 159 yds/50gm skein): grey pearl (MC), 2 (2, 3, 3) skeins, rhodolite (CC), 1 (1, 1, 2) skein(s).

GAUGE: 26 sts + 33 rnds = 4" (10 cm) in patt on larger ndls, after blocking.

NEEDLES: 1 - 16" US 2 (3 mm) circs and set dpns + 1 - 16" + 24" US 3 (3.25 mm) circs and set dpns.

NOTIONS: Tapestry needle, 4 stitch markers, stitch holder, 1 - 1/2" button.

SIZE: NB-6 (6-12, 12-18, 18-24) months.

SKILLS: Colorwork in the round, increasing, decreasing.

Colette

WORTHY OF NOTE: The body and sleeves of Colette are knit in the round and then joined for the raglan yoke. The yoke is worked back and forth for the last few inches to accommodate the larger heads of babies and toddlers. When joining the body and sleeves you may find it helpful to place a contrasting color marker to differentiate the beg of rnd from the raglan decrease markers.

SLEEVE CHART:

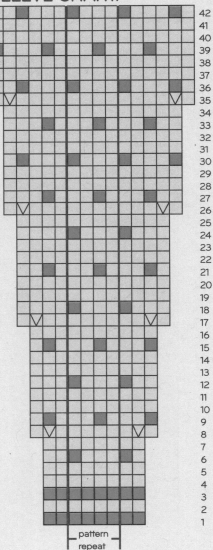

HEART CHART:

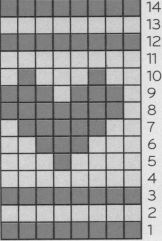

CHART KEY:

- ■ Knit 1 in CC
- ☐ Knit 1 in MC
- ⊻ M1 in MC

LICE CHART:

pattern repeat

DIRECTIONS:

BODY: Hem: Using MC and smaller needles, CO 120 (128, 136, 144) sts. Join for working in the rnd being careful not to twist sts. PM indicating beg of rnd. Work in garter (purl 1 rnd, knit 1 rnd) for 1.25". Knit 1 rnd. **Increase for Body:** Next rnd (inc rnd): *K 15 (16, 17, 18), m1; rep from * around - 128 (136, 144, 152) sts. **Body:** Change to larger 16" circ ndls. Work rnds 1-14 of Heart Chart. Work rnds 1-6 of Lice Chart 4 (4, 6, 8) times, then rnds 1-3 0 (1, 0, 0) time more. Piece should meas appx. 6 (6.5, 7.5, 8)" from CO edge. **Divide for Armholes:** Next rnd: Using MC, knit 70 (74, 78, 84) sts, slide previous 12 sts off of RH ndl onto holder, knit to end, remove m, knit 6, slide previous 12 sts off of RH ndl onto holder - 52 (56, 60, 64) sts each on front and back. Do not break yarn. Leave sts on circ ndl and set aside.

SLEEVES (MAKE 2): Cuff: Using MC and smaller ndls, CO 32 (32, 40, 40) sts. Join for working in the rnd being careful not to twist sts. PM indicating beg of rnd. Work in garter (purl 1 rnd, knit 1 rnd) for 1", ending after working a knit rnd. Knit 1 rnd. **Increase for Sleeve:** Next rnd (inc rnd): *K 8 (4, 10, 5) m1; rep from * around - 36 (40, 44, 48) sts. **Sleeve:** Change to larger ndls. Work rnds 1-42 of Sleeve Chart - 44 (48, 52, 56) sts after all inc's have been worked.

Sizes 12-18 (18-24) only: Work straight in Lice Patt as set until piece meas 7.25 (8.25)" from CO edge, ending after working a rnd 3 or 6 of chart.

Divide for Armholes: Next rnd: Using MC, knit until 6 sts rem, slide next 6 sts onto holder, remove m, slide next 6 sts onto holder - 32 (36, 40, 44) sts rem on ndls. Break yarn.

JOIN BODY + SLEEVES: Using MC yarn from sweater front and 24" circular, knit 52 (56, 60, 64) sts from body front, pm, knit 32 (36, 40, 44) sts from right sleeve, pm, knit 52 (56, 60, 64) sts from back, pm, knit 32 (36, 40, 44) sts from left sleeve, pm indicating beg of rnd - 168 (184, 200, 216) sts. Rnd 1 (CC): Knit all sts. Rnd 2 (MC): Knit all sts. Rep rnds 1 + 2 one (one, two, two) times more.

YOKE: Size NB-6 (6-12) only: Rnd 3 (CC): K2tog, knit until 2 sts before m, ssk, slm; rep from * to end - 8 sts dec'd. Rnd 4 (MC): Knit all sts. Rep rnds 3 + 4 four (six) times more, then rnd 3 once more - 120 (120) sts.

Size 12-18 (18-24) only: Rnd 3 (CC): K2tog, knit until 2 sts before m, ssk, slm; rep from * to end - 8 sts dec'd. Rnd 4 (MC): Knit all sts. Rnd 5 (CC): Knit all sts. Rnd 6 (MC):

Knit all sts. Rep Rnds 3 - 6 two (five) times more, then Rnds 3 + 4 five (three) times more, then rnd 3 once more - 128 (136) sts. **Begin Working Back and Forth (All Sizes):** Row 1 (WS, MC): Purl all sts. Slide ndl to other side to work another WS rnd. Row 2 (WS, CC): *P2togtbl, purl to 2 sts before m, p2tog, slm; rep from * to end - 112 (112, 120, 128) sts. Row 3 (RS, MC): Knit all sts. Slide sts to other side of ndl in order to work another RS row. Row 4 (RS, CC): *K2tog, knit until 2 sts before m, ssk, slm; rep from * to end - 104 (104, 112, 120) sts. Change to MC. Row 5 (WS): Purl all sts. **Begin Working in Garter:** Change to smaller ndls. Row 6 (RS): *K2tog, knit until 2 sts before m, ssk, slm; rep from * to end - 8 sts dec'd. Row 7 (WS): Knit all sts. Rep Rows 6 + 7 two times more then Row 6 once more - 72 (72, 80, 88) sts. Next row (WS): BO all sts knitwise.

FINISHING: Weave in ends. Slide live underarm sts to needles and finish with a 3-needle bind off on WS or kitchener stitch on RS. Soak in cool water and wool wash and block to measurements. Using crochet hook and MC, single crochet around open edge at yoke, make a button loop, sew button opposite loop.

SCHEMATIC:

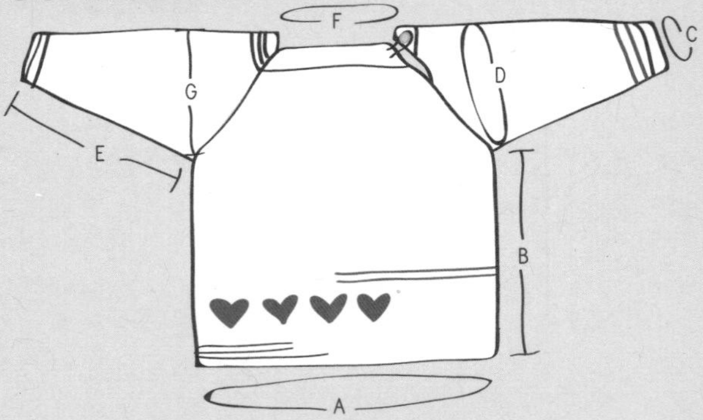

A: 19.75 (21, 22.25, 23.5)"
B: 6 (6.5, 7.5, 8.75)"
C: 5.5 (6, 6.75, 7.5)"
D: 6.75 (7.5, 8, 8.75)"
E: 6.25 (6.25. 7.25, 8.25)"
F: 12 (12, 12.5, 13.5)"
G: 3.5 (4, 5.5, 6)"

Darling

by Courtney Kelley

●●○○

skill level: intermediate

YARN: The Fibre Company Organik (70% organic merino, 15% baby alpaca, 15% silk; 98 yds/ 50 gm skein): aquatic forest, 1 skein or cumulus, 1 skein.

GAUGE: 17 sts + 26 rows = 4" (10 cm) in St st on larger ndls, after blocking.

NEEDLES: 1 pair US 6 (4 mm) straights + 1 pair US 7 (4.5 mm) straights.

NOTIONS: 4 stitch markers, tapestry needle, 2 - 3/4" buttons.

SIZE: To fit NB-6 (6-12) months.

SKILLS: Knitting, purling, increasing, decreasing, short rows.

Darling

WORTHY OF NOTE: Darling is shaped by short-rows. Work the "w+t" and "close" as follows:

W+T (Wrap and Turn):
(RS): Wyib, slip the next st as if to purl from LH to RH ndl, yfwd, Sl st from RH to LH ndl, yarn back, turn.
(WS): Wyif, slip the next st as if to purl from LH to RH ndl, yarn back, Sl st from RH to LH ndl, yarn front, turn.

CLOSE:
(RS): P/u wrap with RH ndl from front to back, knit wrap and the wrapped st tog.
(WS): P/u wrap with RH ndl from back to front, sl wrap from RH to LH ndl. P wrap and wrapped st tog.

DIRECTIONS:
BACK: Ribbing: Using smaller ndls, CO 46 (56) sts. Work in K1, P1 rib for 5 (7) rows.
Work Buttonholes: Next Row (RS): (K1, p1) 2x, k1, yo, k2tog, (p1, k1) to last 7 sts, k2tog, yo, (p1, k1) 2x, p1. Continue in rib as set for 5 (7) rows more, ending after working a WS row. Change to larger ndls. **Body:** Row 1 (RS): Knit all sts. Row 2 (WS): K4, purl to last 4 sts, k4. Rep Rows 1 + 2 2 (4) times more. **Begin Decreases:** (RS): K4, ssk, k to last 6 sts, k2tog, k4 - 2 sts dec'd. Next Row: K4, purl to last 4 sts, k4. Rep previous 2 rows 4 times more - 36 (46) sts. Work straight in patt as set for 6 (8) rows more.

SHORT ROWS PART 1: Row 1 (RS): K to last 7 sts, w+t. Row 2 (WS): Sl1, purl to last 7 sts, w+t. Row 3: Sl1, knit to 4 sts from previous wrap, w+t. Row 4: Sl1, purl to 4 sts from previous wrap, w+t. Rep Rows 3 + 4 once (twice) more - 6 (8) center sts between the wraps. Next row (RS): Sl1, knit to end, closing all gaps created by turn. Next Row (WS): K4, purl to 4 sts rem, k4, closing all gaps.

SHORT ROWS PART 2: Row 1 (RS): K21, (26) sts, w+t. Row 2 (WS): P6, w+t. Row 3: K6, close, k3, w+t. Row 4: P10, close, p3, w+t. Row 5: K14, close, k3, w+t. Row 6: P18, close, p3, w+t.

Small size only: Row 7: K22, close, k6. Row 8: K4, p25, close, p2, k4.

Large size only: Row 7: K22, close, k6, w+t. Row 8: P29, close, p6, w+t. Row 9: K36, close, k to end. Row 10: K4, p37, close, k4.

FRONT: Begin Decreases: Row 1 (RS): K4, ssk, knit to last 6 sts, k2tog, k4 - 2 sts dec'd. Row 2 (WS): K4, p2tog, purl to last 6 sts, ssptbl, k4 - 2 sts dec'd. Rep Rows 1 + 2 three times more - 20 (30) sts. **Begin Increases:** Row 1 (RS): K4, m1R, k to last 4 sts, m1L, k4 - 2 sts inc'd. Row 2: Knit 4, purl to last 4 sts, k4. Rep Rows 1 + 2 3 times more - 28 (38) sts. Work straight in patt as set for 12 (16) rows.

RIBBING: Change to smaller needle and work 11 (15) rows in K1, P1 rib.

FINISHING: Bind off all sts in patt. Weave in ends. Soak in cool water and wool wash and block to measurements. Sew buttons opposite buttonholes.

SCHEMATIC:

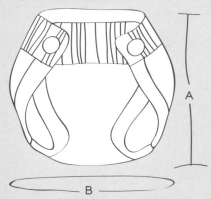

A: 6.5 (8)"
B: 14 (18.5)"

Finley

by Courtney Kelley

● ● ○ ○

skill level: intermediate

YARN: The Fibre Company Savannah (50% wool, 30% cotton, 15% linen 15% soya; 160 yds/50gm skein): natural, 2 skeins.

GAUGE: 25 sts + 32 rnds = 4" (10 cm) in double moss st on larger ndls, after blocking.

NEEDLES: 1 - 16" US 4 (3.5 mm) circs and set dpns + 1 - 16" US 5 (3.75 mm) circs and set dpns.

NOTIONS: Tapestry needle, 2 stitch markers, waste yarn or stitch holder.

SIZE: NB-6 (6-12, 12-18) months.

SKILLS: Working flat and in the round, increasing, decreasing.

Finley

WORTHY OF NOTE: Finley is knit seamlessly in the round from the waist to the cuff. In order to maintain a seamless stitch pattern while increasing, K1b and P1b increases are worked. Please make sure to read through all abbreviations before beginning.

DIRECTIONS:

Waist: Using smaller ndls, CO 86 (118, 134) sts. Join for working in the rnd, being careful not to twist sts. PM indicating beg of rnd. Work in k1, p1 rib for 2". **Inseam:** Change to larger ndls. Work rnds 1-4 of Moss Stitch 7 (9, 10) times then work rnds 1 + 2 once more, working last rnd as follows: work in patt for 43 (59, 67) sts pm, work in patt to end. **Increase for Gusset:** Rnd 1: K1b, *p1, k1; rep from * to 1 st before m, p1, m1k, slm, p1b, *k1, p1; rep from * to last st, k1, m1p - 4 sts inc'd. Rnd 2: *K1, p1; rep from * to end. Rnd 3: *P1, k1; rep from * to end. Rnd 4: *P1, k1; rep from * to end. Rnd 5: P1b, *k1, p1; rep from *to 1 st before m, k1, m1p, slm, k1b, *p1, k1; rep from * to 1 st before m, p1, m1k - 4 sts inc'd. Rnd 6: *P1, k1; rep from * to end. Rnd 7: *K1, p1; rep from * to end. Rnd 8: *K1, p1; rep from * to end. Repeat rnds 1-8 1 (2, 3) times more, then rnds 1-7 once more - 110 (150, 174) sts.

DIVIDE FOR LEGS: Work 55 (75, 87) sts in patt as set to m, remove m(s) and place rem 55 (75, 87) sts on holder. Work each leg separately.

LEGS: CO 1 st using loop method - 56 (76, 88) sts. This is the new beg of rnd. Cont in patt as set, using larger dpns and without increasing, for 3 (3, 5) more rnds. Begin dec every 4th rnd maintaining patt as follows: Rnd 1: Work in patt to one st before end of rnd, slip next stitch onto lh ndl, k(p)3tog as necessary to maintain patt. Rnds 2-4: Work 3 rnds even in patt as set. Rep rnds 1-4 9 (13, 15) times more — 36 (48, 56) sts. Work straight in patt until leg meas 5.5 (7.5, 9)". Change to smaller dpns and work in k1, p1 rib for 1.5". Bind off loosely. Repeat for second leg.

FINISHING: Weave in ends. Soak in cool water and wool wash and block to measurements.

SCHEMATIC:

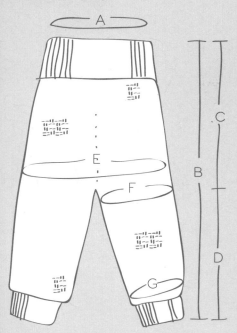

A: 13.75 (19, 21.5)"
B: 15.75 (19.75, 22.75)"
C: 8.75 (10.75, 12.25)"
D: 7 (9, 10.5)"
E: 17.5 (24, 27.75)"
F: 9 (12, 14)"
G: 5.75 (7.75, 9)"

Florence

by Kate Gagnon Osborn

● ● ○ ○

skill level: intermediate

YARN: The Fibre Company Canopy Worsted (50% baby alpaca, 30% merino, 20% viscose from bamboo; 200 yds/50gm skein): quetzal, 1 skein.

GAUGE: 20 sts + 40 rows = 4" (10 cm) in garter st, after blocking. 1 Lace pattern repeat (11 sts) = 2.125".

NEEDLES: 1 - 16" US 5 (3.75 mm) circs and set dpns.

NOTIONS: Tapestry needle, 2 stitch markers.

SIZE: To fit babies 4-12 months. Cap: 14" circ and 7.25" high, Bootie: 3.5" length, 6" circ.

SKILLS: Knitting lace, i-cord, increasing, decreasing.

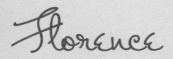

Florence

WORTHY OF NOTE: The cap begins with an i-cord tie; stitches are then picked up to work the body. A small tab is then worked, stitches are picked up, and then the body is joined for working in the round for the decreases at the back.

The booties are worked from the sole to the cuff. The soles are worked back and forth, then stitches are picked up to work the side of the foot. Short rows are then worked for the top of the bootie, and are finished with a rib and garter cuff.

CHART KEY:

- ☐ K on RS, P on WS
- ⊟ P on RS, K on WS
- ▐ Sl1
- ◿ K2tog
- ◺ ssk
- ⊙ YO

LACE CHART:

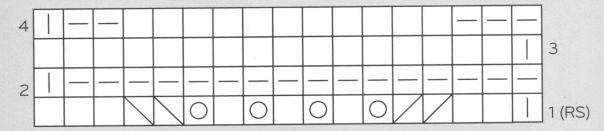

I-CORD: CO 4 sts onto dpn. Rnd 1: K4, slide sts from left to right side of ndl. Do not turn. Pull working yarn in preparation to work another rnd. Rep Rnd 1 to specified length.

LACE PATTERN (worked flat over a multiple of 11 sts + 6): Row 1 (RS): Sl1wyib, k2, *k2tog, k2tog, (yo, k1) 3x, yo, ssk, ssk; rep from * to 3 sts rem, k3. Row 2 (WS): Sl1wyib, knit to end. Row 3: Sl1wyib, knit to end. Row 4: Sl1wyib, k2, purl to 3 sts rem, k3. Rep rows 1-4 for patt.

CAP DIRECTIONS: I-CORD TIE: Using dpns, CO 4 sts. Work in I-Cord for 50 rnds, pm, work in I-Cord for 72 rnds, pm, work in I-Cord for 50 rnds, BO all sts, break yarn. I-Cord should meas appx. 30" long.

CAP: Using circ ndl and starting at m, pick up and knit 72 sts inbetween ms on I-Cord - 72 sts on ndls. Work in garter stitch for 6 rows. Next row (WS): Sl1, k2, purl to 3 sts rem, k3. Work Rows 1-4 of Lace Pattern from Chart or written instructions six times. **Garter Tab at Back of Crown:** Row 1 (RS): BO 2 sts, slip st from rh ndl to lh ndl, k3tog, k2tog, (yo, k1) three times, yo, ssk, ssk, *k2tog, k2tog, (yo, k1) three times, yo, ssk, ssk; rep from * to 3 sts rem, k3. Row 2: Sl1, k2, turn. Rep row 2 thirteen times more. BO 3 sts, break yarn. **Join for Working in the Round:** Beg at start of garter tab, pick up and knit 7 sts along edge, pm indicating beg of rnd - 73 sts. **Back of Crown Decreases:** Rnd 1: Purl all sts. Rnds 2 + 3: Knit all sts. Rnd 4: *K2tog, k7, ssk; rep from * to 7 sts rem, k7 - 61 sts. Rnd 5: Purl all sts. Rnds 6 + 7: Knit all sts. Rnd 8: *K2tog, k5, ssk; rep from * to 7 sts rem, k7 - 49 sts. Rnd 9: Purl all sts. Rnds 10 + 11: Knit all sts. Rnd 12: *K2tog, k3, ssk; rep from * to end - 35 sts. Rnd 13: Purl all sts. Rnds 14 + 15: Knit all sts. Rnd 16: *K2tog, k1, ssk; rep from * to end - 21 sts. Rnd 17: Purl all sts. Rnds 18 + 19: Knit all sts. Rnd 20: *S2KP; rep from * around - 7 sts.

FINISHING: Break yarn. Thread through live sts and fasten. Using ends, seam garter tab at back. Weave in remaining ends. Block piece to measurements.

BOOTIE DIRECTIONS: SOLE: CO 5 sts. Row 1: K1f+b, k2, k1f+b, k1 - 7 sts. Rows 2 + 4: Knit all sts. Row 3: K1f+b, k4, k1f+b, k1 - 9 sts. Row 5: K1f+b, k6, k1f+b, k1 - 11 sts. Knit 13 rows. Row 19: K1, SKP, k to 3 sts rem, k2tog, k1 - 2 sts dec'd. Knit 5 rows. Row 25: K1, SKP, k to 3 sts rem, k2tog, k1 - 2 sts dec'd. Knit 5 rows. Row 31: K1, SKP, k to 3 sts rem, k2tog, k1 - 2 sts dec'd - 5 sts.

INSTEP: Rnd 1: K5, p/u and knit 16 sts

across side of foot, pick up and knit 5 sts across toe, pick up and knit 16 sts across side of foot, pm indicating beg of rnd - 42 sts. Rnds 2, 4, 6: Purl all sts. Rnds 3, 5: Knit all sts.

TOP OF BOOTIE:
Row 1: Knit 22, k1f+b, k1f+b, k1, ssk, turn. Row 2: Sl1wyif as if to purl, p5, p2tog, turn. Row 3: Sl1wyib as if to knit, k2, yo, k1, yo, k2, ssk, turn. Row 4: Sl1wyif as if to purl, k7, p2tog, turn. Row 5: Sl1wyib as if to knit, k1f+b, k4, k1f+b, k1, skp, turn. Row 6: Sl1wyif as if to purl, p9, p2tog, turn. Row 7: Sl1wyib as if to knit, k2tog, (k1, yo) 4x, k1, (skp) 2x, turn. Row 8: Sl1wyif as if to purl, k11, p2tog, turn. Row 9: Sl1wyib as if to knit, k11, skp, turn. Row 10: Sl1wyif as if to purl, p11, p2tog, turn. Row 11: Sl1wyib as if to knit, k2tog, k2tog, (yo, k1) 3x, yo, (ssk) 3x, turn. Rep Rows 8-11 two times then Row 8 once more - 30 sts after all rows have been worked. **Decrease for Cuff and Return to Working In the Round:** Sl1 as if to knit, k11, skp, k5, slm, p10, k2tog, k12, p5 - 28 sts. Next rnd: Knit all sts.

CUFF:
Work in k1, p1 rib for 8 rnds. Work in garter st for 12 rnds. BO all sts kwise.

FINISHING:
Break yarn, weave in ends. Fold garter portion of cuff over ribbing.

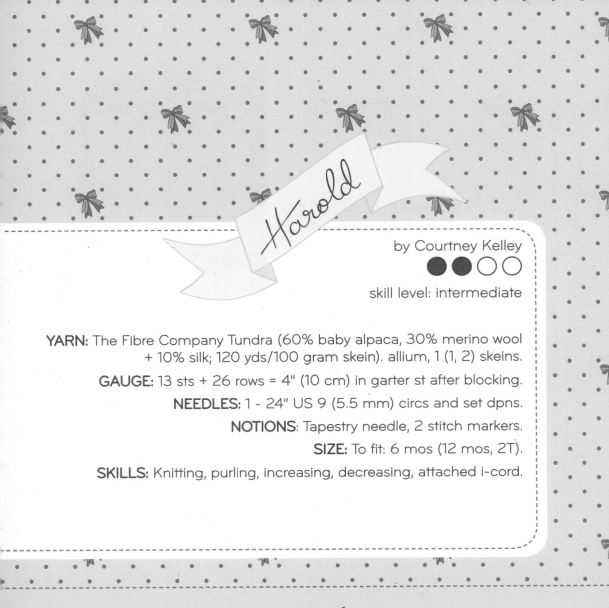

Harold

by Courtney Kelley

skill level: intermediate

YARN: The Fibre Company Tundra (60% baby alpaca, 30% merino wool + 10% silk; 120 yds/100 gram skein). allium, 1 (1, 2) skeins.

GAUGE: 13 sts + 26 rows = 4" (10 cm) in garter st after blocking.

NEEDLES: 1 - 24" US 9 (5.5 mm) circs and set dpns.

NOTIONS: Tapestry needle, 2 stitch markers.

SIZE: To fit: 6 mos (12 mos, 2T).

SKILLS: Knitting, purling, increasing, decreasing, attached i-cord.

Harold

WORTHY OF NOTE: Harold is worked with an integrated I-Cord around all edges, and is finished at the shoulders with a 3-needle I-Cord bind off. The body is knit in one piece, beginning at the back and increasing both fronts as you work. Warm and cozy this is a great bit of outerwear for your little one.

I-CORD: Rnd 1: K3, slide sts from left to right side of ndl. Do not turn. Pull working yarn in preparation to work another rnd. Rep Rnd 1 to specified length.

3-NEEDLE I-CORD BIND OFF: Row 1: K2, k3tog (2 sts from front ndl with 1 st from back ndl), sl3 sts back onto LH ndl. Pull working yarn around back in preparation to work another RS row. Rep Row 1 for bind off.

DIRECTIONS:

BACK: Hem: Using provisional cast-on method of your choice and circ ndls, CO 3 sts. Work in I-Cord for 48 (54, 60) rnds. Turn I-Cord 90 degrees and p/u and knit 48 (54, 60) sts (1 st in each rnd) along top of I-Cord. Remove provisional CO and

place 3 sts onto RH needle - 54 (60, 66) sts. **Body:** Row 1 (WS): Sl3 wyif, knit to last 3 sts, s3 wyif. Row 2 (RS): K3, k1f+b, k to last 5 sts, k1f+b, k4 - 2 sts inc'd. Rep prev 2 Rows 11 (13, 15) times more, then Row 1 once more - 78 (88, 98) sts. **Work Buttonhole:** Next Row (RS): K3, BO2, knit to end. Next Row (WS): Sl3 wyif, k to bound off sts and cast on 2 sts using backwards loop method, sl3 wyif. **Divide for Fronts and Back:** Row 1: Knit 21 (25, 29), turn. Place remaining 57 (63, 69) sts on holder. Row 2: Sl3 wyif, knit to last 3 sts, s3 wyif.

RIGHT FRONT: Decrease for Neck and Armholes: Row 1: K3, ssk, k to last 5 sts, k2tog, k3 - 2 sts dec'd. Row 2: Sl3 wyif, knit to last 3 sts, s3wyif. Rep Rows 1 + 2 two times more - 15 (19, 23) sts. **Decrease for Neck:** Row 1: K3, ssk, k to end - 1 st dec'd. Row 2: Sl3wyif, knit to last 3 sts, s3wyif. Rep Rows 1 + 2 6 (8, 10) times more - 8 (10, 12) sts. Place sts on holder. Break yarn.

BACK: Place 36 (38, 40) back sts on ndls, leaving 21 (25, 29) left front sts on holder. Join yarn, ready to work a RS row. Row 1: Knit all sts. Row 2: Sl3wyif, knit to last 3 sts, s3wyif. **Decrease for Armholes:** Row 1: K3, ssk, knit to last 5 sts, k2tog, k3. Row 2: Sl3wyif, knit to last 3 sts, s3wyif. Rep Rows 1

+ 2 two times more - 30 (32, 34) sts. Work straight in patt as set for 12 (16, 20) rows more. Place sts on holder. Break yarn.

LEFT FRONT: Place 21 (25, 29) left front sts on ndls, join yarn, ready to work a RS row. Row 1: Knit all sts. Row 2: Sl3wyif, knit to last 3 sts, s3wyif. **Decrease for Neck and Armholes:** Row 1: K3, ssk, k to last 5 sts, k2tog, k3 - 2 sts dec'd. Row 2: Sl3wyif, knit to last 3 sts, s3wyif. Rep rows 1 + 2 two times more - 15 (19, 23) sts. **Decrease for Neck:** Row 1: Knit to last 5 sts, k2tog, k3 - 1 st dec'd. Row 2: Sl3wyif, knit to last 3 sts, s3wyif. Rep rows 1 + 2 6 (8, 10) times more - 8 (10, 12) sts. Place sts on holder. Do not break yarn.

SHOULDERS: Place held back sts on circ ndls, and left and right front sts on separate dpns. Fold fronts to close vest with WS facing each other. With RS facing you, using yarn attached to left front, CO 3 sts onto dpn holding L front sts, using cable or knit cast-on. Work Row 1 of the 3-Needle I-Cord Bind Off until 8 (10, 12) left front sts have been bound off. Sl rem 3 sts onto LH ndl for back and work I-Cord bind off as follows: *K2, k2tog, sl 3 sts onto LH ndl; rep from * until 8 (10, 12) back sts rem. Work 3-needle I-Cord bind off across rem back and right sts. Fasten off.

FINISHING: Weave in ends. Soak in cool water and wool wash and block to measurements. Sew button opposite buttonhole.

- -

SCHEMATIC:

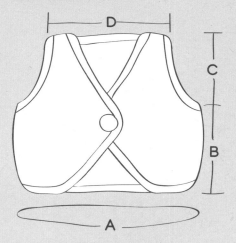

A: 20.5 (23.5, 26.75)"
B: 7 (8, 9)"
C: 5.25 (6.25, 7.5)"
D: 9.25 (10, 10.5)"

Mollie

by Courtney Kelley

● ● ○ ○

skill level: intermediate

YARN: The Fibre Company Canopy Fingering (50% baby alpaca, 30% merino, 20% viscose from bamboo; 200 yds/50gm skein): palm bud, 2 skeins.

GAUGE: 27 sts + 37 rnds = 4" (10 cm) in St st, after blocking.

NEEDLES: 1 - 16 US 1 (2.5 mm) circs., US B (2.25 mm) crochet hook.

NOTIONS: Tapestry needle, 2 stitch markers, 2 - ½" buttons, 2 yds -¼" satin ribbon.

SIZE: One size, 20.75" circ at widest point and 13.5" length to armhole: to fit most newborns.

SKILLS: Knitting flat and in the round, decreasing.

Mollie

WORTHY OF NOTE: The size of the Mollie can be adjusted slightly by changing gauge. A gauge of 32 sts/4" will give a chest circumference of 13" and a gauge of 28 sts/4" will give a chest circumference of 15". Canopy Fingering will beautifully accommodate this range of gauges.

DIRECTIONS: BODY: CO 140 sts. Join for working in the rnd, being careful not to twist sts, PM indicating beg of rnd. Work in K2, P2 rib for .75". Eyelet rnd: *K3, k2tog, yo; rep from * to end. Work in St st until piece meas 8" from cast on edge, working last rnd as follows: Knit 70, pm, knit to end. Next rnd (dec rnd): *K1, ssk, knit to 3 sts before m, k2tog, k1, slm; rep from * to end - 4 sts dec'd. Knit 3 rnds even. Rep prev 4 rnds 8 times more - 104 sts after all dec's have been worked. Work in St st until body measures 13.5" from cast on edge.

DIVIDE FOR ARMHOLE: Set-up: Knit until 5 sts before m, BO 10 sts, removing m as you come to it, knit to 5 sts before eor m, BO 10 sts, removing marker as you come to it - 42 sts each side.

Work back and fronts back and forth separately in garter stitch.

FRONT YOKE: Work in garter stitch until yoke meas 1.5". Bind off for neck: Knit 12, BO 18, knit to end. Work each shoulder strap separately. Dec at neck edge every RS row 2 times - 10 sts. Knit 8 rows. Bind off all sts. Repeat for other shoulder.

BACK YOKE: Work in garter stitch until yoke meas 2". Bind off for neck: Knit 10, BO 22, knit to end. Work each shoulder strap separately. Knit 14 rows. Work buttonhole: K3, k2tog, yo, knit to end. Knit 4 rows. Bind off all sts. Repeat for other shoulder.

CROCHET EDGE AT YOKE: Using crochet hook and yarn, work a row of single crochet around neckline and armholes.

FINISHING: Sew buttons to front straps to match placement of buttonholes. Weave in ends. Soak in cool water and wool wash and block to measurements. Thread ribbon through eyelets, beginning at center front of garment; trim ribbon to desired length.

Mildred

by Kate Gagnon Osborn

skill level: intermediate

YARN: The Fibre Company Terra (40% baby alpaca, 40% merino, 20% silk; 98 yds/50gm skein): mint, 2 (2, 3, 3, 4) skeins.

GAUGE: 17 sts + 32 rnds = 4" (10 cm) in Garter St, after blocking.

NEEDLES: 1 - 16" US 7 (4.5 mm) circs and set dpns.

NOTIONS: Tapestry needle, stitch marker, cable needle, 1 - 34" button.

SIZE: NB-6 (6-12, 12-18, 18-24, 24-36, 36-48) months.

SKILLS: Garter stitch in the round, basic cables.

Mildred

WORTHY OF NOTE: The vest is worked in the round and then divided for the armholes. The fronts are then worked back and forth to the shoulders. In order to hide the jog that occurs when working garter in the round, the eor is placed at the center front right before the cable.

CABLE PATTERN:
Rnd 1: C10F, knit to end.
Rnds 2, 4, 6, 8, 10: K10, purl to end.
Rnds 3, 5, 7, 9: Knit all sts.

DIRECTIONS: BODY: Using circs, CO 76 (84, 94, 98, 102, 106) sts. Join for working in the rnd, being careful not to twist sts. PM indicating beg of rnd. Set-Up: Rnd 1: Knit all sts. Rnd 2: K8, purl to end. Rep Rnds 1 + 2 three times more. **Begin Working Cables:** Rnd 1: Sl 4 sts to cn, hold front, k4, k4 from cn, knit to end. Rnd 2: K3, k1f+b, m1, K4, purl to end - 78 (86, 96, 100, 104, 108) sts. Rnd 3: Knit all sts. Rnd 4: K10, purl to end. Repeat rnds 3+4 three times more. **Body:** Work rnds 1-10 of Cable Pattern 3 (4, 5, 5, 6, 6) times, then rnds 1-4 once more. Piece

should meas appx 5.5 (6.75, 8, 8, 9.25, 9.25)" from CO edge.

DIVIDE FOR ARMHOLES: Row 1: Knit 22 (24, 27, 28, 29, 30) sts, BO6, knit 32 (36, 40, 42, 44, 46) sts, BO6, knit 12 (14, 17, 18, 19, 20) sts to end, remove m - 34 (38, 44, 46, 48, 50) sts rem on front, 32 (36, 40, 42, 44, 46) sts rem on back. Break yarn. Transfer front sts to st holder.

BACK: Join yarn in preparation to work a WS row. Row 1 (WS): Sl1 wyib, knit to end. Row 2 (RS): Sl1 wyib, ssk, knit to 3 sts rem, k2tog, k1 - 2 sts dec'd. Rep Rows 1 and 2 two times more - 26 (30, 34, 36, 38, 40) sts. Work straight in garter, as set until vest meas 3 (3.5, 3.75, 4, 4.5, 5)" from division for armholes, ending after knitting a WS row. Break yarn. Transfer live sts to holder.

FRONT: Transfer live sts to ndls. Join yarn in preparation to work a WS row. Row 1 (WS): Sl1 wyib, k11 (13, 16, 17, 18, 19), p10, k to end. Row 2: Sl1 wyib, skp, knit to 3 sts rem, k2tog, k1 - 2 sts dec'd. Row 3: Sl1 wyib, k10 (12, 15, 16, 17, 18), p10, k to end. Row 4: Sl1 wyib, ssk, knit to 3 sts rem, k2tog, k1 - 2 sts dec'd. Row 5: Sl1 wyib, k9 (11, 14, 15, 16, 17), p10, k to end. Row 6: Sl1 wyib, ssk, k7 (9, 12, 13, 14, 15), sl 5 sts to cn, hold front, k5, k5 from cn,

knit to 3 sts rem, k2tog, k1 - 28 (32, 38, 40, 42, 44) sts. Row 7: Sl1 wyib, k8 (10, 13, 14, 15, 16), p10, k to end. **Divide for left and right:** Row 1 (RS): Sl1 wyib, k7 (9, 12, 13, 14, 15), k2tog, k4, place rem sts (right front sts) on holder, turn - 13 (15, 18, 19, 20, 21) sts rem on ndls.

LEFT FRONT: Next Row (and all remaining WS rows): Sl5 wyif, knit to end. **Decrease for Neck Edge:** Dec 1 st at neck edge every other row 2 (3, 4, 4, 4, 4) times, then every 4th row 1 (2, 2, 2, 2, 2) time(s) as follows: Sl1 wyib, knit until 6 sts rem, k2tog, k4 - 10 (10, 12, 13, 14, 15) sts rem after all dec's have been worked. Work straight until left front meas 3.5 (4, 4.25, 4.5, 5, 5.5)" from start of armhole shaping, ending after knitting a WS row. **Make Buttonhole:** Sl1 wyib, k1 (1, 2, 3, 3, 4), k2tog, yo, knit to end. Work 4 rows straight in pattern as set. BO all sts knitwise.

RIGHT FRONT: Join yarn in preparation to work a WS row. **Decrease for Neck Edge:** Dec 1 st at neck edge every other row 2 (3, 4, 4, 4, 4) times, then every 4th row 1 (2, 2, 2, 2, 2) time(s) as follows: Sl1 wyib, knit until 6 sts rem, p2togtbl, p4. Work all other (non-decrease) WS rows as follows: Sl1 wyib, knit to 5 sts rem, p5. Next Row (and all remaining RS rows): Sl5 sts wyif, knit to end - 10

(10, 12, 13, 14, 15) sts rem after all dec's have been worked. Work straight as set until left front meas 3 (3.5, 3.75, 4, 4.5, 5)" from start of armhole shaping, ending after working a WS row.

JOIN SHOULDERS: Transfer back sts to spare size 7 circ. Fold work so RS of right front and back face one another. Using dpns, BO 4 (4, 6, 7, 8, 9) sts using three-needle bind-off, knit 5 sts from right front - 6 sts rem on ndls for front, 21 (25, 29, 31, 33, 35) sts rem on back. Flip work back so RS of front is facing. Work attached i-cord across back neck: *Slide sts from left to right in preparation to work i-cord. K4, sl1 as if to knit, k1 from back, psso; rep from * until all back sts have been worked - 5 sts rem. BO all sts.

FINISHING: Weave in ends, block. Soak in cool water and woolwash, pin to measurements and let dry. Sew button to back left shoulder opposite buttonhole.

SCHEMATIC:

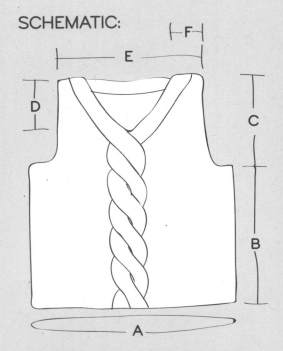

A: 17.5 (19.5, 21.5, 22.5, 23.5, 24.5)"
B: 5.5 (6.25, 7.5, 7.5, 8.75, 8.75)"
C: 3 (3.5, 3.75, 4, 4.5, 5)"
D: 2 (2.5, 2.75, 3, 3.5)"
E: 6 (7, 8, 8.5, 9, 9.5)"
F: 1.5 (1.5, 2.25, 2.5, 2.75, 3)"

Nellie

by Kate Gagnon Osborn

skill level: intermediate

YARN: The Fibre Company Organik (70% organic merino, 15% baby alpaca, 15% silk; 98 yds/50 gm skein): cumulus (MC), 4 (4, 5, 6) skeins, crater lake (CC1) + arctic tundra (CC2), 1 skein each.

GAUGE: 19 sts + 25 rnds = 4" (10 cm) on larger ndls in St st, after blocking.

NEEDLES: 1 - 24" US 7 (3.25 mm) circ and set dpns + 1 - 16" Size 5 (3.5 mm) circ and set dpns.

NOTIONS: 4 stitch markers, tapestry needle, 8 (10, 13, 14) - 1/2" buttons.

SIZE: To fit NB-6 (6-12, 12-18, 18-24) months.

SKILLS: Increasing, decreasing, picking up stitches.

Nellie

WORTHY OF NOTE: Ollie is worked in one piece from the bottom up. After the legs are joined and the body is established, stitches are bound off for the front and you will finish working back and forth. Sleeves are worked in the round and then joined for the raglan yoke. Once the yoke is complete, stitches are then picked up to work the buttonbands.

STRIPE PATTERN:
Rnds 1-3 (CC2): Knit all sts.
Rnds 4-5 (MC): Knit all sts.
Rnd 6 (MC): K1, m1R, knit to one st before m, m1L, k1 - 2 sts inc'd.
Rnds 7-9 (CC1): Knit all sts.
Rnds 10-11 (CC2): Knit all sts.
Rnd 12 (CC2): K1, m1R, knit to one st before m, m1L, k1 - 2 sts inc'd.

DIRECTIONS: LEGS (MAKE 2): Cuff:
Using CC1 and smaller ndls, CO 38 (38, 40, 40) sts. Join for working in the rnd, being careful not to twist sts. Work in k1, p1 rib for 1.75". **Begin Stripe Pattern:** Change to larger ndls and work rnds 1-12 of stripe patt - 42 (42, 44, 44) sts. Change to MC. Knit 5 (5, 3, 3) rnds even. Next rnd (inc rnd): K1, m1R, knit to one st before m, m1L, k1 - 2 sts inc'd. Rep previous 6 (6, 4, 4) rnds 3 (4, 6, 8) times more - 50 (52, 58, 62) sts. Work straight until leg meas 7 (8, 10, 11)" from CO edge, working last rnd as follows: Knit to end, remove m, k4, slide 8 sts from RH ndl onto holder - 42 (44, 50, 54) sts rem on ndls. Break yarn on left leg. Do not break yarn on right leg.

JOIN LEGS + WORK BODY: Using 24" circ, knit 42 (44, 50, 54) sts from right leg, pm, knit 42 (44, 50, 54) sts from left leg, pm - 84 (88, 100, 108) sts on ndls. Knit 3 rnds. **Increase for back:** Next rnd (inc rnd): Knit until 2 sts before 1st m, m1R, k2, slm, k2, m1L, knit to end - 2 sts inc'd. Knit 3 rnds. Next rnd (inc rnd): Knit until 3 sts before 1st m, m1R, k3, slm, k3, m1L, knit to end - 88 (92, 104, 112) sts. **Divide for buttonband and begin working back and forth:** Knit until 2 sts rem, BO2, remove eor m, BO2 - 84 (88, 100, 108) sts. Work 2 rows in St st. Next Row (inc row, RS): Knit until 4 sts before m, m1R, k4, slm, k4, m1L, knit to end- 2 sts inc'd. Work 3 rows in St st. Next Row (inc row, RS): Knit until 5 sts before m, m1R, k5, slm, k5, m1L, knit to end- 2 sts inc'd. Work 3 rows in St st. Next row (inc row, RS): Knit until 6 sts before m, m1R, k6, slm, k6, m1L, knit to end

- 2 sts inc'd - 90 (94, 108, 114) sts. Work straight until piece meas 14.5 (17, 21, 23)" from CO edge, ending after working a WS row as follows: Purl 26 (26, 31, 32) sts, slide 8 sts from RH ndl onto holder, purl 46 (50, 54, 58) sts, slide 8 sts from RH ndl onto holder, purl 18 (18, 23, 24) sts to end - 74 (78, 92, 54) sts rem on ndls, 18 (18, 23, 24) sts for each front and 38 (42, 46, 50) sts for back. Do not break yarn.

SLEEVES: Using smaller ndls and CC1, CO 26 (28, 30, 32) sts. Join for working in the rnd, being careful not to twist sts. PM indicating beg of rnd. Work in k1, p1 rib for 1". Change to larger ndls and work rnds 1-12 of stripe patt - 30 (32, 34, 36) sts. Change to MC. Knit 4 rnds even. Next rnd (inc rnd): K1, m1R, knit to one st before m, m1L, k1 - 2 sts inc'd. Rep previous 5 rnds 3 (3, 5, 6) times more - 38 (40, 46, 50) sts. Work straight until sleeve meas 6 (6.5, 8, 9)" from CO edge, working last rnd (RS) as follows: Knit to end, remove m, k4, slide 8 sts from RH ndl onto holder - 30 (32, 38, 42) sts rem on ndls.

JOIN BODY + SLEEVES: Row 1 (RS): Knit 18 (18, 23, 24) sts from right front, pm, 30 (32, 38, 42) sts from right sleeve, pm, 38 (42, 46, 50) sts from back, pm, 30 (32, 38, 42) sts from left sleeve, pm, and 18 (18, 23, 24) sts from left front - 134 (142, 168, 182) sts. Row 2 (WS): Purl all sts. Sizes (12-18, 18-24) only: Work 4 rows in St st. **Begin Raglan Decreases:** Row 1 (RS, dec row): Knit to 2 sts before m, ssk, slm, k1, k2tog; rep from * 3 times more, knit to end - 8 sts dec'd. Row 2 (WS): Purl all sts. Rep Rows 1+2 9 (10, 15, 17) times more - 54 (54, 56, 62) sts. Change to smaller needles

NECK RIBBING: Row 1 (Set-Up, RS): K2, (p1, k1); rep from * 11 (11, 11, 14) times, p2tog, **(K1, p1); rep from ** to 2 sts rem, k2 - 53 (53, 55, 61) sts. Row 2 (WS): P2, *(k1, p1); rep from * to 1 st rem, p1. Work in patt as set until ribbing meas 1". BO all sts in patt.

BUTTONBANDS: Left Buttonband: Starting at neck edge with RS facing and using smaller ndls, pu and knit 51 (61, 77, 85) sts along left front edge. Row 1 (WS): *P1, k1; rep from * to 1 st rem, p1. Row 2 (RS): *K1, p1; rep from * to 1 st rem, k1. Row 3 (RS, buttonhole row): K1, p1, k1, yo, *(p1, k1) 3 times, yo; rep from * 6 (8, 11, 12) times more, (p1, k1) to end. Row 4: *Work in rib as set to 1 st before yo, k2tog; rep from * to 3 sts rem, p1, k1, p1. Work in rib as set for 2 rows. BO all sts in patt. **Right Buttonband:** Starting at bottom edge with RS facing and using smaller ndls, p/u and knit 51 (61, 77, 85) sts along right front edge. Row 1 (WS): *P1, k1; rep from * to 1 st rem, p1. Row 2 (RS): *K1, p1; rep from * to 1 st rem, k1. Work in rib as set for 4 rows more. BO all sts in patt.

FINISHING: Graft underarm sts or finish with 3-needle bind off. Weave in ends. Soak in cool water and wool wash and block to measurements. Sew buttons opposite buttonholes.

SCHEMATIC:

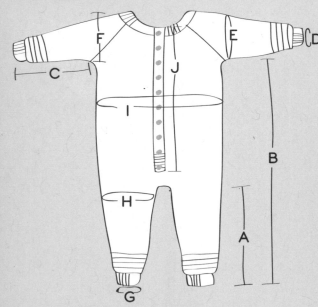

A: 7 (8, 10, 11)"
B: 14.5 (17, 21, 23)"
C: 6 (6.5, 8, 9)"
D: 5.5 (5.75, 6.25, 6.75)"
E: 8 (8.5, 9.5, 10.5)"
F: 3.5 (4, 5.5, 6)"
G: 8 (8, 8.5, 8.5)"
H: 10.5 (11, 12.25, 13)"
I: 20 (20.75, 23.75, 25)"
J: 11 (13, 16.5, 18)"

Odette

by Grace Anna Farrow

skill level: intermediate

YARN: The Fibre Company Canopy Fingering (50% baby alpaca, 30% merino, 20% viscose from bamboo; 200 yds/50gm skein): orchid, 4 skeins.

GAUGE: 20 sts + 36 rnds = 4" (10 cm) in St st, after blocking.

NEEDLES: 1 - 24" US 4 (3.5 mm) circs and set dpns.

NOTIONS: Tapestry needle, 4 locking stitch markers.

SIZE: 30" square.

SKILLS: Knitting flat and in the round, decreasing.

Odette

WORTHY OF NOTE: Odette is worked from the center out on dpns. You will move to the circular needle when the circumference is too large to fit comfortably on the dpns. Place a marker on the stitch indicated, not in between the stitches. You may find it helpful to use a different (color or type) marker for the beginning of the round. The markers at the 25th, 49th, and 73rd sts are located in the center of the 8 yarn overs that create the corners of the blanket.

DIRECTIONS:

SET-UP: Using your preferred method, circularly cast on 8 sts. Join for working in the rnd, being careful not to twist sts. PM indicating 1st stitch of rnd. Rnd 1: *K1, yo; rep from * around - 16 sts. Rnds 2+3: Knit all sts. Rnd 4: *K1, yo; rep from * around - 32 sts. Rnds 5-8: Knit all sts. Rnd 9: *K1, yo; rep from * around - 64 sts. Rnds 10-16: Knit all sts. Rnd 17: (K1, yo) 4 times, *k8, (k1, yo) 8 times; repeat from * to 12 sts rem, k8, (k1, yo) 4 times - 96 sts. Mark the 25th, 49th, and 73rd stitches with markers.

BODY: Rnds 1-7: Knit all sts. Rnd 8: (K1, yo) 4 times, *k to 3 sts before the m'd st, (yo, k1) 3 times, yo, knit m'd st, [yo, k1] 4 times; rep from * two times more, knit to last 4 sts, (k1, yo) 4 times - 32 sts inc'd. Work rnds 1-8 thirteen times more - 544 sts.

HEM: Rnds 1-7: Knit all sts. Rnd 8: *Yo, k2tog; rep from * around. Rnds 9-15: Knit all sts.

FINISHING: Bind off all stitches using large dpn, attaching hem to WS of blanket as you go as follows: Insert RH ndl into st on LH ndl and into the corresponding purl bump on the WS of the blanket, knit tog the LH st and the purl bump and complete the bind off. Weave in ends. Soak in cool water and wool wash and block to measurements.

Abbreviations:

BO: bind off
circ: circumference
C10F: Sl 5 sts to cn, hold front, k5, k5 from cn
cn: cable needle
CC: contrast color
CO: cast-on
dec'd: decreased
dec(s): decrease(s)
dpn(s): double pointed needle(s)
eor: end of row/round
inc'd: increased
inc(s): increase(s)
K: knit
K1b: knit into the st below the next st on your lh ndl - 1 st inc'd
k1f+b: knit one into the front and back of the same stitch - 1 st inc'd
k2tog: knit 2 sts together - 1 st dec'd
LH: left hand
m(s): marker(s)
m1R/L: make 1 right/left - 1 st inc'd
MC: main color
meas: measures
ndl(s): needle(s)

P: purl
P1b: purl into the st below the next st on your lh ndl - 1 st inc'd
P2togtbl: purl 2 sts together through the back loop - 1 st dec'd
PM: place marker
p/u: pick up
patt: pattern
rem: remain / remaining
rep: repeat
RH: right hand
rnd(s): round(s)
RS: right side
Sl: slip
Sl2KP: slip 2 sts tog kwise, k1, psso - 2 sts dec'd
ssk: slip, slip knit - 1 st dec'd

GARTER STITCH (worked flat):
Row 1: Sl1, knit to end
Rep row 1 for pattern

MOSS STITCH (worked in the rnd):
Rnds 1+2: *K1, p1; rep from * to end
Rnds 3+4: *P1, k1; rep from * to end

SOURCES:

All of the yarns in this book are from The Fibre Company and are distributed by Kelbourne Woolens.
For stockist information, please visit: www.thefibreco.com/retailers.html

Contact info@kelbournewoolens.com for inquiries on patterns or the Fibre Company yarns.

OUR YARNS:

Each yarn in The Fibre Company lineup is the product of thoughtful fiber selection for the best results in stitch definition, colorwork, cables, and lace. We favor the kettle dyeing method for its depth of color and subtle heathered tones. Our unique fiber blends absorb the dye in different ways, creating a beautiful dimensionality that is the hallmark of The Fibre Company yarns.

SUPPORT:

Keep updated with Kelbourne Woolens through our blog: kelbournewoolens.com/blog, follow us on Instagram, like us on Facebook, and join the Kelbourne Woolens and I Heart the Fibre Company groups on Ravelry.com to share your projects.

IN GRATITUDE:

There are many people who deserve our heartfelt thanks for helping us with the success of Kelbourne Woolens, continued growth of the Fibre Company, and for making this book possible. To Daphne and Iain: thank you, forever and always. To our amazing sample knitter, Deirdre: you're awesome. To our tech editor, Laura, our proofreader Sara, and our support team at Puritan: your attention to detail is amazing. And to our KW Team: Maura, Leah + Meghan: you rock.